MY COUNTRY

MY COUNTRY

★ ★ ★

BY RUSSELL W. DAVENPORT

NEW YORK 1944

SIMON AND SCHUSTER

SECOND PRINTING

MANUFACTURED IN THE UNITED STATES OF AMERICA

This song belongs to my mother

Cornelia Whipple Davenport

who taught me to cherish freedom

MY COUNTRY

·I·

AMERICA is not a land of ease.
We have not paused from action to beget
Heroic simile and song and frieze;
We have no empire of the mind as yet,
Nor have we shed our light within the grave:
But, as the sons of enterprise and sweat,
Honor the quick, the strong, the free, the brave—
The mind whose thoughts are cradled in the hand—
The fierce emancipators of the slave
Exacting destiny of virgin land.
We are the builders of dynamic things,
Successors to the spires of Samarkand—
Boilers and bars, propellers, wheels and wings
To run and fly and dive at our behest,
Through which the mighty wind of freedom sings.
America is not a land of rest.

None is released, as lover in the night,
Upon the mystic cadence of her breast,
Whether as paramour or parasite,
Or has of her the Lotus-wine of sleep;
For only in the day does she delight,
The open eyes, the heart unsatisfied,
The urge to risk, to fabricate, to reap—
And windy prairielands, horizon-wide,
And cloudy streams from which the salmon leap.
We are the men of motion and desire,
Spirits that seek, engender, and collide
Like atoms of regenerating fire:
The western men who must forever be
Consumed in deeds, to which their souls aspire;
The bright, creative fuel of destiny
That burns in action as in ecstasy.

America is generous to the free:
To those who ask no favor of the great,
And grant them none, except equality;
The masters, not the minions, of the state:
To him who gives no margin to the snob,

But thinks and breathes as freedom's delegate
Against the fashion or the gathering mob.
All tongues and races are American,
All nations are embodied in her job,
To breed the noble concept of a man
Whose freedom is, that others should be free—
Yellow or black or red or white or tan.
This was the burden of the prophecy,
When from the wharves of Boston, and the whips,
There rose the blessed words of liberty
Upon the rebel pens and patriot lips:
And she was ever generous to those
Who saw her first as promise from the ships,
The empty-handed and contemned, who chose
To risk the towering glamor of her shore;
Italians, Slavs, and Jews, the "dese and dose"
Who came with song and fiddle and guitar;
And those of Spain and Crete and Singapore
In pants of blue and shawls of cinnabar;
And those of Ayr and Cork; and those who bore
In them the scars of Pinsk and Bucharest,
The dusty orts of kaiser, king, and czar,
Which still she gathered to her mighty breast:

Whereon the light of liberty sufficed
To make their hidden splendor manifest—
And every jewel among them equal-priced
By her own law, as in the Word of Christ.

My country loves the lovers of her land:
They who in Spring behind the heavy plows
Rip up the sterile project Winter planned;
When brooks are like extended veins, and sloughs
Have soaked the feet of every shivering hill,
And in the April sunlight Winter's cows
Crop the intoxicating chlorophyll:
They who endure the agony, who share
The lustful intumescence of the Will
To wake the larvae and enchant the fair
And wistful flowers from the dark, and call
The butterflies into the dusty air
And orange honeysuckle from the wall;
And the muscled Will of pregnancy to squeeze
From deep and planetary silence, all
That life has yet conceived, or can increase;
To load the land with hay and golden grain

And vines and heavy corn and calves and pease,

In light as hot as liquor in the brain,

In August when the sun goes down so late;

And willow trees, reflective and sedate,

And crimson apples like the dreams of gain:

Or yet those others, restless ones, who boast

Some secret kinship with the course of fate,

Who haunt the hills with Summer's screaming ghost

When the New England trees disintegrate

Like incantations chanted to the frost,

And all the jewelry of her land is lost,

Of which in summertime she was so fond,

And carried outward on the beat of drums—

The wings of wild geese far above the pond.

These men she loves: and those who see beyond

The blindness of the earth when Winter comes,

When all the house is cluttered with its gear

And children squirm and struggle with their sums

Year after year

Beside the fire that hisses as its goes;

The lean, far-sighted countrymen who hear

The breath of living things beneath the snows,

And feel the hope of Heaven in their blood,

And far below the frost, the glowing Rose.

The earthy men are those

Who have America to love and keep:

Her mountaintops, her daring clouds that scud

Above the dappled carpets that we reap;

Her rain, her snow, her forest-fire, her flood,

Her dusty winds, her tidal hurricanes,

Her desert buttes, her lakes, blue-eyed and deep,

Her foaming rocks and shores, her silver veins.

These are her men, to whom she will confide

The secret of the seed that she contains,

Which has so generously multiplied

Within the fertile pastures of her creed;

The seed of liberty, which can provide,

Out of the dark and frozen depths of need,

The love of man, the Flower of the freed.

Yet freedom is no life

Of elegance and graceful mood:

The breed of freedom is a breed of strife,

Restless and rude,

Reared to the earthy struggle of its time.

Only the thought of freedom is sublime,
Its flesh is knit of discord and of feud
Among a people hardened by their skills:
Of racket, labor riot, sex, and crime,
The dark, glimmering clash of wills—
Colliding waves   destroyer of itself:
The ruse
          the squint
                    the insolent drawling

Eye to eye
          a pistol on a shelf:

The thing that looks
                    that horrifies
                              that kills
In hate
          in Hagerstown and Pawling:

The pulsing focus of the soul   the self
The self is freedom
                    ever-lustful
                              brawling:
Exponent of the struggle for survival
The conqueror of beast   by beast   by beast
Wary   rapacious   rampant   and salival
Through the forgotten forests of the East:

This brute, this mammaled memory of the sea,
Evolving in the frenzy of the chase,
In drums and bloody dances 'round the priest,
In spoliage, in conquest, race by race;
This self in search of its entelechy,
With all the jungle written in its face:
This is the thing America makes free.

And there are the clean muscles also; the bright
Clean wings of transports leaping from the field;
The hard, clean fight
Of men well matched and angry for the right;
The clean, transparent power of a wheel
Driven by the invisible and profound;
The sound
Of rivet-hammers hitting the clean steel
Dominantly, in the high naves
Of yards where the red ships are keeled;
The clean click of the drives
Over the bright green fairways, after work;
The clean girls laughing on the merry-go-round
And through the park . . .
The evident, the positive, the seen,

The bright, the clear, the hard, the diamond-ground,
The clean—
Such is the will of those who struggle here
In mind and muscle, motion and machine:
Lawyer and carpenter and engineer,
Bricklayer, seamstress, bolter, go-between,
The salesman and the beautiful cashier;
The zealous people avid to pursue
The protean American Career;
The lovers of the daring and the new—
Competitive, impacked and numberless:
The apostles of American success,
The priests of the Pursuit of Happiness.

Yet to what purpose freed?
                    By what mutations
To reach what ultimate
                    to fill what need?
By what light to proceed?
                    What intimations?
What answers give
                    to the beast enfranchised?
Questions
        and questions
                    and speculations
For which we are not yet experienced

Not yet American-ripe
       not positive:

Only
    we feel the urge
       we live

Only living
    feeling that we live

Here
    with a Constitution we devised

For the aspiring
      the competitive:

And if there is some magic in our land,

As on Darien surmised;

Some distant purpose hidden in the hand,

Some ultimate fulfillment of the free

Beyond collision and rapacity—

It is that there incarnates in the beast

A Spirit native to the universe,

Which by our signature we have released,

Beyond recall, from human custody:

That we endure no bondage to rehearse

The mummery of autocrat or priest,

And so have liberated from the curse

Of servitude, as from the thrall of sin,

The glowing seed of God that lives within.

Strong men these are, whose hearts can never rest;

Forever ending, only to begin;

Forever moving on the trackless quest

Of what forever is, yet cannot be:

Forever turned to face the arduous West—

The dream of progress to infinity—

The eternal destination of the free.

· II ·

AND yet it is not clear   not clear   not clear
    Darkness is all around us   and the cries
Of dying men   and fear   and other fear:
The fear of eyes staring at other eyes,
Of eyes that stare at nothing to be seen,
Or at Nothing in disguise—
Pumpkins in the dark of Hallowe'en:
The Jewish threat   the Catholic   the Black
Bureaucrat   labor leader   pacifist
Tycoon   appeaser   egomaniac
And nihilist—
The fears that flourish in the other fears
Hammer-and-sickle   swastika   fascine
And Hitler . . .
Yes, there are things to fear
(But let us fear the ones that there are
To fear
            let us fear
                        only in freedom's name) . . .

Fear the image of man in steel and motion
The iron image   the carborundum
Image   the hope of man   in aluminum
The dream in cement of man with electric thoughts
The copper nerves   the brass guts   the bars
Impassioned as men are   the wheels turning
Like the thoughts of men   and the fires   and the white pig
Spouting from the bellies   and the red blooms
Rolled and rerolled   longer and longer
To the shape of a man's ambition . . .

There is this blind thing,
There is this thing grown
Out of us—this thing:
Thing of energy,
Thing of steel, of speed—
Blind—infinitely
Strong and swift and blind:
Not God's thing, not God's
Thing, but man's—man's thing:
Thing without soul—the
Dead thing living—thing
Evolving out of

The beast-flesh without
The soul of the beast:
The huge thing that moves,
The thing that moves all,
That moves always and
All together in
Unison always:
The thing without breath
Without eyes without
Ears without sleep—life
Without life or death:
This is the lathe turning,
This is the drill, this is
The planer planing, this
The jig, the dictator,
The indispensable;
This is the cutter cutting,
This is the feeder feeding,
This is the gear-box, this is
The slab-cutter, this is the
Go-gauge and this the Not-go:
This is the micrometer to
One-thousandth, this is the Vernier

To the ten-thousandth, these are the
Drop forgings for the heart—the dead heart:
These are the substances of the dead—
The living dead, the animated dead,
The nickel steel dead, the chrome steel dead, the
Hard steel dead, the carbide, the cobalt:
The "high-shock, fatigue-resisting" never-tired
Dead thing created in the image of man.
No never tired
                    never tired
                                never tired . . .
The bright machines
                    the lovely

Bright incredible machines:

The goddesses of mind
                    of space and time
The turning goddesses
                    the heartless
Goddesses
            the living-dead
                        the breathless goddesses:
These are the vampire goddesses
                                the vampires
The glistening destroyers
                    the revolving

Goddesses
   the heartless goddesses
The lovely goddesses
    the bright incredible
Machines . . .
Living in motion to destroy the living:
Living among the living without God.

Let us not fear Man: let us fear
Only what he believes in.
The red dirt falls over Birmingham, on the houses
Where the niggers lie in the darkness
     waiting for freedom:
And the workers of Pontiac and the River Rouge
      wait for the
Clear vision:
   and in Manhattan they climb
The stairs in the evening
    seeking it
     and the elevators
Slide up and down behind the lights
     sighing
And the people in them sigh
    for the lost dream.
Have we found it in Chicago by the blue lake?

Have we found it where the streets run interminably

Through the passions of man
                              or on the flats

Where the monsters are that consume the remains

Of another age?
                    Or on the infinite stoops of

West Philadelphia
                    have we found it?

Or under the unseeing sky of Boston
                                        or over

The gutted hills of Butte
                            or the teeming hills

Of Seattle:
            the vision
                        the dream of a new freedom?

Or have we

Found it in the promised land, the far country

Where the rivers used to wind through the hills
                                                like lovers?

Youghiogheny   Monongahela   Ohio.

But the hills are dead now and the slag spewed

Into the valleys where the reeds were and the willows,

And the rivers are empty of fish and their desire is

For Nothing:
                and the dream has gone out of this land

And the houses cling to the dead hills as children

To the memory of God . . .
                                        O my country,

It is Nothing that we must fear: the thought of Nothing:

The sound of Nothing in our hearts
                                        like the hideous scream

Of fire-engines in the streets at midnight:

The belief in Nothing.

Here are the signs of Nothing and the portents,

Where the machines are, and their priests
                                        and their prophets:

Where the fire is, and only

Fire: and cinders and only cinders:

And the voices rising up from the cities, where

The people are—but only voices . . .

Let us search, then:

Let us search in the void where God is

(If anywhere): let us search in the blackness:

Search the universes beyond the universe,

And the atoms within us and the forces

Within the atoms: give us instruments,

Give us tools—the bright, arcane

Tools of the mind: the wires, the beams of light,

The tubes, electrons, needles, particles,

Waves, grids, condensers, slides, and super-film:

Maybe we can find God now

With the electronic microscope

In the invisibly intimate; or maybe

In the stars with a colossal

Telescope in California:

Give us theodolites and spectroscopes,

Telepolariscopes and ammeters

And gyroscopes and galvanometers

And polarimeters and chronographs:

Give us all—everything that weighs

Or measures, everything that compares,

Posits, checks, balances, responds:

Everything that can refract or bend;

Everything that can reflect, transpose,

Compute, divide, react, and segregate:

Let them be infinitely accurate,

Let them be infinitely sensitive—

Lest we fail
            lest somehow we miss it

Lest we miss God
            fail to see Him

Fail to weigh Him
            fail to measure Him

Fail to probe where He is:
                    fail
To probe beyond Nothing:
                        fail to find
Anything beyond Nothing
                    anything where
                                God is

Where God is . . .
                where God is . . .

Oh, the instruments:
Oh, the bright tools made
Of mind—the new mind—
Mind extended:
Mind of measurement,
Mind of steel, of glass—
Blind—infinitely
Intricate and blind:
Not God's mind, not God's
Mind, but man's—man's mind—
Metal mind without
Eyes—the fireless mind—
The dead mind of the
Living—mind of death:

These are the extensions
Created without soul
By the beast, created
Of the beast, for the beast,
In the hands of the beast:
Inanimate extensions
Of the beast—extensions of
Man the ever-extending,
The evolving-in-water
Through-the-air on-earth under
Above around by over
Across with of into and
In the infinitely finite:
Unknown and relative to the
Unknown and relative to the
Related and still relative
To the unrelated, the presumed . . .
(Oh, where is the presumed?
                    Oh, where is

The uncreated place?)
                    Where is God?

Where is He?
            Where?
                    Where?

Not in the instruments:
                    not in
The telescopes
                    the microscopes
The spectroscopes
                    the chromatometers
The calorimeters
                    the carbonometers
Not in these
            Oh
                    not in these reflections
These rediscoveries of ourselves within
The instruments
                    ourselves
In the extension of ourselves:
                            No
                                not
In these encounters with ourselves
                            beyond
Ourselves
            the meeting of the mind
                                beyond
The mind
            the meeting of ourselves
                                beyond
Where the mind is
                in darkness
                            where

We are
      in Nothing
            rediscovered
By Nothing
        in the blackness
              of Nothing
To believe in Nothing
           to be Nothing
               Nothing
Nothing . . .

We have found Nothing:
We have seen it, have
Seen Nothing—the face
Of Nothing—we know
Nothing, we have heard
Nothing, heard it rant,
Heard it proclaim the
New Order of Hate,
The Godless Order:
The radio face
In the darkness of hate
Where man ends who
Is without freedom,

Is the machine-man,
The instrument-man,
The automatic
Man without soul—where
Man is without God:
Not God's face, not God's
Face, but man's—man's face,
The man-face without
Love, the machine-face
The instrument-face
Without faith without
Hope—man-face without
Christ, the Anti-Christ:
These are the Poles dying,
These are the Czechs, these are
The dead Jews, these the
French running, these the
Fair cities of Holland
Burning, these the British
Driven into the sea:
These are the Yugoslavs
Crushed, these the Greeks starving,
These the Russians falling

In snow by the million

Before the machine-face:

These are the shattering bombs,

These the women, the wailing

Babies, the timbers falling,

Roofs spouting, stone walls crumbling,

Glass crashing, bodies flying,

Beds, rags, running feet, fire,

Water, blood
          silence:
               and the burnt

Faces—and the dawn—the gray dawn

Moving into the desolate cities

Moving into the desolate streets and

Over the hearts of people looking   over

The people   over the looking people for

People in silence lost and forever buried

Under the buildings
              under the Nothing.

This is the face—
         this—
              now we have seen it

Now we have seen the face
              looked into the eyes:

Now we know what fear is
                    what the price is

What pain is
           what fear is

What hate is
           what blood is

What fear is
           what death is:

Now we know that it hurts
                that freedom hurts

Oh, God it hurts
             O God
                   It hurts buddy

Oh, Christ save me
            Oh, help

Oh, Jesus
          This is more than I can take

O Christ
       O God . . .
             O Jesus . . .

·III·

Here lies an American soldier:
He is dead.

There is no blood in his hollow cheek,
In his twisted hand there is no nerve,
He is dead.

Who among us will speak for this man,
Who will say what there is to be said?
Who will set forth what the dead deserve
Concerning the dead?

It is not easy for us to speak:
In the empty heart there is no song,
There is no light in the eyeless head:
There are no words in a cynic world
To honor the dead.

Among his countrymen who will speak?
Who will say what there is to be said
In behalf of the dead?

HIS SISTER SPEAKS:

"When Pop got the telegram he didn't know what to
do.

It was just after noon and Pop had come in to wash
up for dinner and Mom was in the kitchen and she
hollered to Pop to answer the door and it was the
telegram.

I was standing there in the hall and I watched him
read it and then I watched him just stand there:

He didn't know what to do.

Then he kind of crumbled it in his hand and he turned
with his head bowed and put one foot on the stairs
and held on to the banister:

And then he just went upstairs, slow, like a great
weight, and then I thought I knew what it was and
I was scared and began to cry:

But I didn't know what to do, either.

So I just stood there: and then without thinking I ran
up the stairs after Pop and went right in:

And Pop was sitting there on the edge of the bed with
his knees spread wide apart and his hands holding
on to the edge and the telegram crunched up under
one hand:

And he looked at me when I came in—he just looked.
And then he said, 'Hello, Sis . . . Hello, Kid,' he
said.

He didn't know what to do.

'Is it—?' I said. 'Is it—?' And he just nodded his head slow and held out the telegram and I took it.

But I couldn't read it. I just saw 'Adjutant General' and then I saw backward until I saw 'KILLED IN ACTION':

Then I couldn't see anything at all.

'We've got to tell Mom,' Pop said. 'We've got to tell Mom.'

And I thought, 'Poor Pop—poor old Pop.' And then I thought, 'Gee, he wants me to help him. He didn't say "I," he said "we." He wants me to help him.'

But I didn't know what to do.

So I just turned and looked out the window down the valley toward where the river goes into the willows:

And I saw our pasture, where it comes down out of the woodlot, and I saw our meadow as bright green as May in the sun:

And I looked at the stone wall that Larry had fixed when he was a kid and the stile he'd made so's Mom could get to the orchard easy:

And I looked down through the window of the shed and I saw Larry's motorcycle propped up and the sun was shining on it through the window:

And the breeze came in from around the back of the house and I smelled the blossoms of the old crabapple the way it was when we were kids and used to pretend it was jasmine:

And I turned around to Pop and just let myself down
   onto his knees and cried . . . and cried . . . and
   cried . . ."

In the heart, when the dread word reaches into the
                                       homes of America,
That he who was there like the sun has departed forever,
Then sorrow falls as the night over the secret places
Of memory and of laughter,
And the hungry shadows of death enclose the living.
What shall we say to those who have lost their soldiers?
What light have we to show, what words, beyond
                                            their tears?
There were Americans once who believed in God,
But we are the unbelievers, the darkened people;
We are the generations who have lost the faith.

We have had a vision of man, an American dream
Of man augmented by his infinite works:
Creature of new extensions, ever-emerging,
Spirit in many shapes, ever-evolving:
The appointed and transcendent animal,
Multiplied in its faculties, winged and wheeled,

Wired, propelled, lighted, electronized
To see in the dark of the earth, hear in the silence,
Measure and weigh and touch the unattained.
This is the vision of man as superman,
Stretched to the great horizons of the mind.
But what have we had of this? The dream
Has ended in horror: the hope falls
With our sons on the acrid battlefields of the world.
There is a Shape within,
A howling Shape of sheds and smoking-pits,
A blind and monstrous Image of ourselves,
Faithless to all and ignorant of love.
This is the kinematic golden calf,
In whose obedience we have created hell
More terrible on the face of the earth than that
Which was presumed to await us in the grave;
Wherein the power of every evil is raised
By engines and designs to higher powers,
And the warm flesh, in our bewildered lives,
Becomes the agent of Satanic appetites—
Rage, hate, slaughter—mass-produced,
Many-levered and malevolent—
Pregnant with wars that are, and are to be.

Oh, it is in us, the evil!

In us the evil grew—engendered

Evil behind the pious and empty mask

Of pacifism and hypocrisy.

Where was America, in the name of God,

When all the broken-hearted world was waiting

For us to act? We could have risen then:

Risen against ravishment and theft

In China and Ethiopia—murder

In Spain—doubt in the sad, shaken streets—

Passions oozing from Berlin—lies,

Cynic insolence, disclosures, hate—

Betrayal of honor, contract, law, justice,

Free speech, and peace.

We could have risen: yet we did not rise.

We were neutral!—

Neutral with the light on our faces

Of bonfires burning up our destiny:

Neutral to torture, murder, rape; neutral

As death toward our deluded sons

Who fell in the tangled gullies of the Argonne,

Of whom we did not ask neutrality.

They lie there now, betrayed, under crosses

Emblazoned with names from Pennsylvania,
Kentucky, Maine, California—
Danish and Italian boys—Irish—Armenian—
Our boys, thrust from all around the earth
Into those cemeteries, where, instead of freedom,
Their monument was the German infantry.
We did not end their war.
We failed to make their peace, or in their name
To rebuild the ruined prospects of mankind:
Failed to prevent the re-engendering
Of hate and horror—even to prepare—
Even to face our own necessities.
We did nothing. We were neutral. No—
We would rather be pushed around by bastards
From Tokyo and Berlin, and have our flag
Smeared by the spittle of our conquerors,
Our boys captured, starved, dismembered,
Our islands overpowered, our creed of freedom
Prostituted in the alleys of the mind;
And suffer all the indignities of men
Without the will to be what they believe—
Rather all this, than to arise in time
Against our known and natural enemies.

And now we have one cry—the ancient cry:
More boys—more boys—more boys!
Throw them against the beaches! Hurl them
Into the reckless ruins of Italy!
Let them be blown to bits by bombs and rockets,
Submerged in the sea and frozen in the ice,
Their eyes lost, their legs, their testicles;
Their lives scrambled and their hopes deferred:
And all for us, whose greed and cowardice
Nourished the human monsters that they fight.
More boys—more boys—more boys!

How should we speak of death, except as death?
Where is the light of love and resurrection?
Our gods are stolen from the depths of matter,
And they have led us into the desolate country,
They have betrayed us into the wasted land.
How should we illuminate—
How resurrect
Truth from the empty skulls strewn along
The riverbeds of the past, which have no water?
Sister of death, weep: weep for your soldier.
There is nothing else to do, nothing to be said.

The sun is on our land, but nothing grows.
The bones of Christ are scattered across the rocks.
The rocks are marked with the feet of other ages.
God is not anywhere. And the springs of love
Are empty . . .

But here an American soldier
Is lying dead.

There is no blood in the hollow cheek,
There is no light in the darkened nerve,
Or in the head.

Is there none in our midst who can speak?—
None to say what there is to be said?
None to set forth what the dead deserve
Concerning the dead?

Lest he lie forever, killed in vain,
Lost in the dust of the wasted land,
Dead as the shape of his hollow cheek,
Oh, speak, countrymen! . . . . .
Speak!

HIS TEACHER SPEAKS:

"There is almost nothing I can say . . .

A memorial service will be held at the Presbyterian Church next Sunday: the whole school will attend.

I suggest also that those of you who knew him, write to his parents and his sister . . . any little word . . .

Of course there is nothing that anyone can say . . .

But before placing this first gold star on our school service flag perhaps it is fitting to remind ourselves:

To remind ourselves of Larry in action, for he loved action;

To remind ourselves of Larry on the football field; for there he was at home.

I do not know how he was killed: but I think of him as thrusting forward, as on our Memorial Field,

I think of him as thrusting forward with that amazing confidence of his; I think that is the way it must have been, giving everything he had:

He was a very generous boy.

And for my part I want to say that I believe that Larry died for a reason, that he died for a cause:

I believe that he died for freedom.

I don't mean that he was thinking about freedom—I doubt if he was thinking about anything except the enemy.

And I am sure that if ever he thought about freedom

out there in the foxholes it was never the way we learn about freedom here in books.

When he thought about freedom he thought about you sitting here, his friends;

He thought about our town, and the life we lead here, and the fun we have, and the good things we have to eat, and the bright hopes that we all share:

These, I am sure, were Larry's idea of freedom.

But as his former teacher I want to point out that this life of ours, this free life, is not the result of accident.

Freedom as we live it here in America is an inheritance from ages past;

Freedom is a spark, whose origin is lost in ancient times;

A spark that was nourished in Athens, in the Acropolis, in the debates of those days and the productions of the immortal philosophers and dramatists;

A spark that was fanned to flame in Galilee by Him who announced the great and single law of freedom, that men should love each other.

Thereafter this flame survived through dark and dangerous centuries,

And emerged in England, where common men like you and me learned how to assert their rights against the power of kings:

And from England this flame was carried across the

Atlantic and lighted in the great, dark forests of the New World.

And so it was by no mere accident that Larry was called to go out and fight against the declared enemies of freedom:

He fought, not just to avenge Pearl Harbor, not just for our security, and not for conquest:

He fought for all that has been gained since men began to record their history—

For all that has been gained, and all that can be gained, and all that will be gained.

He fought that you whose lives still lie before you may have a chance to carry forward,

To carry forward in your lives those long and illustrious gains—

Those gains which men with freedom in their hearts have made against the enemies of man and the enemies of God.

Larry has passed you the ball. Don't let him down!

Take it! Press it to you! Advance it! Run with it!

He was—a generous boy. . . ."

O land of freedom! Spacious hope of man!

Where are the brave, God-given words that woke

The shadowy wilderness to liberty?

Where is that common faith of which we built,

Here on the broad foundation of your shores,
A temple for a human brotherhood?
It was the land which taught us to be free—
The unexpected land that broke the spell
Of Europe on the crowded hearts of men.
For when that stubborn Genoese set sail
From Palos in the glassy dawn, he reached
For empire, in the name of Aragon,
Unknowing that there lay ahead of him
The hills and valleys of a greater reach
Across the ocean of humanity.
"Tierra! Tierra!"—none knew what it meant:
The hidden thought of freedom, leading us
Up the seductive streams to breed our hopes,
And from the Appalachians stretching out,
Always as land, more hopeful, more desired,
Into the brooding Mississippi plain
Where the tracks were of Spaniards and of French;
And on into the country of the sage,
And through the yellow desert and the thirst,
To stand at last upon the western range
And see that other ocean opening out,
As blue as heaven, to the unforetold.

All this we freed: to any man the price
Was only his own courage. And thus the land,
Which hitherto had imprisoned men, became
The school for freedom, where we learned in action
The principles and the million rules that knit
The life of liberty: to keep the doors
Safe from authority, the churches free,
The village greens at peace, the chosen corners
Open for gossip or for diatribe:
And learned to print what we believe, and change
Our minds, and equally maintain another's
Right to be mistaken and his chance
To advocate that which we know is false:
And learned the lean, imperishable truths
Of imperfection; that freedom is designed
To fit the hearts of men, and not of gods;
That justice is uncertain in its course,
And mercy blind, and wisdom too obscure
To earn for any citizen the right
Of undebated power: and learned, therefore,
To check the would-be saviours and the terms
Of officers, however strong or good.
So from the massive freedom of the land

There grew the massive doctrine of the free,
That truth in men is relative to truth
In other men: and no one owns the source
Of that which lights the cities of the mind.

And now the earth is tested, and its peoples
Everywhere: in tiny, ravished Europe,
Or the clear, green hills of Szechwan:
And on the crowded Indus, and along
The tundra shores of unfrequented seas;
The test is here; in noisy Mediterranean
Alleys, and down the Congo where the drums
Beat out the news of armies from the West;
And on the palmed Australian isles, and in
The proud, uncertain lands of Bolivar.
This is the age of which the prophets tell:
In every sea, on every continent
The time has come for freedom—or for death.
O mighty land! Awaken in our hearts
The ancient Spirit, now relaxed in sleep,
Of Liberty, which once inspired our lives:
That we may rise from our enchanted soil
Against the unnatural powers of our time,

And with candescent policies, apply—
Wherever on the earth our name is known—
The universal lessons that we learned
In this majestic and abundant school:
The principles, the rights, the obligations,
The deep and holy structure of our law
Beyond the reach of mere majorities.
These are like water hidden in the hills—
The eternal springs of liberty, whose source,
Though lost beneath the deserts of our time,
Might yet be redivined and opened up
And sluiced into the future of the world.

But here lies on the alien shore
An American soldier.

He lies in the darkness of the dead;
He lies in a grave beyond the latch
Of a secret door.

Who can see what there is to be seen?
Who can say what there is to be said?
Who can compose a last dispatch
From the alien shore?

None of us here in his home can speak,

And none who have known him heretofore:

There is no faith in our hearts, to catch

The knob of the door.

Who is there living among the dead

To open a crack and tell us more?

Who will bring word of our soldier son

From the alien shore?

Speak, countryman, speak,

And open the door!

HIS BUDDY SPEAKS:

"It might just as well have been me.

We're all huddled there under the bank that rises up from the beach to where the bastards're waitin' for us;

And they have an emplacement up there and they're pottin' us with a coupla mortars;

And the Louie says, 'For Crissake we gotta get them sons of bitches outa there. We'll just die like pigs, here,' he says. 'Who'll go up and get 'em?'

So Larry steps up and he says, 'I will, sir.' And because I always went with Larry, I said I would too.

But I'm scared. No kiddin'.

So we climb that there bank.

I ain't never stood naked on Main Street, but that's the way I feel up there, except it's lead comin' at you instead of just people starin';

And I guess it's right there I make up my mind I'm gonna get it, because it's easier that way than tryin' to expect to live in all that lead.

Anyways, Larry starts like he's gonna take on the whole goddam army:

He must be six or eight yards ahead of me and I see him take a grenade, and I see his arm go back to throw it:

Then it's the damnedest thing I ever felt.

I see that grenade lobbin' through the air, and I see Larry fall, like he didn't have any legs. He just falls.

But I swear to God I don't know whether it's him or me that's hit. It might just as well have been me. Anyways, I fall, too.

I don't remember nothin' then:

I must've chucked all my pineapples because when the Louie comes up he says, 'Fine work, Carlson,' he says, 'nice job.'

I'm kneelin' there beside Larry, lookin' at his face, and when the Louie says that it hits me hard;

Because when I hear the Louie use my name like that, then I know I'm alive:

And I look down to Larry, and then I know he's dead,
    not me; and I just put my head down onto his chest
    and blubber like a goddam kid.

I've thought about it in the night a lot of times. It
    might just as well have been me.

Nobody'll ever take away that feelin' I had about
    Larry when I got mixed up;

And for my money that's what the chaplain was
    talkin' about before we got into them lousy barges:
    I never seen it so clear before, and I guess I never
    will again.

And ever since then I've had an idea: I guess maybe
    I'm a bit off my nut, the way you get, but the idea
    keeps comin' back and comin' back, and I wish I
    could express it.

The idea is that when I got mixed up that way between
    Larry and myself—well, that's the goddam way it
    is;

And the idea is that if you could see it that way all the
    time, mixed up like that, the world would be a hell
    of a lot different—

That's the idea.

But you gotta look at it a long time, like it is when a
    flare falls in the night: you have to wait.

And I guess I won't ever be able to express it very
    well . . .

All I can say is there's somethin' we don't see most
  of the time, except in times like that: I know it like
  I'm sittin' here—

Because it might just as well have been me."

On the shore where the stiff white crosses mark
                       a design for eternity,

And the infantry of sleep is forever enrolled in silence,

And the lives of men are but numbers, and an alien wind

Comes up to the beaches, caressing

The fallen sons of men of a distant country:

Here, at last, the meaning and truth of freedom

Opens, unsealed, before the eyes of the nations;

Where death has merged the memories
                       of Maine and Nebraska,

Of Indian fires in the desert, of bearded live-oaks,

The motion of Texas grass when the wind is moving,

The dusty roads that lead to the schools and churches.

Here they merge like a stream—ranches and orchards,

Courthouses, banks, shops, railroads, and factories,

Memories of faces, of lips parted with passion,

Of hands like sunlight on the nerves, of hair fallen

Over the shoulders of someone beyond the ocean.

Here in the name of freedom all have been gathered
Into the perfect union of purposes disunited—
A brotherhood of men in the arms of death
Who were never aware, in life, that they were brothers.
Read the unsealed message, you who desire freedom—
You millions and millions who struggle against each other!
Open these graves to discover
The secret of liberty shoveled under the earth:
Behind the curtain of flesh, as under the crosses,
There is one Brother of all; and all are One.

As in the night,
When a new wind rises out of the hills of America,
The odors of the land are released from secret places
And mists are pulled from the valleys and serious stars
Assemble, as if elected
To represent above us the thought of freedom:
So now, out of the graves,
The boys return to our hearts, like shadows of ourselves;
They are shaped into life again, as moonlight is shaped
By the magic trunks of the white-oaks in tangled woodlots—
Changed as the moonlight is by the brooks into silver,
To reinhabit the land where they cannot live.

Now in the brotherhood of the dead we can see

All who have known her well, all who have loved her,

Who are with her no more in the shape
of their hands or their faces,

But are in us forever a part of her being:

Trappers and tillers, workers, dim representatives,

Heroes who died for the living, who lived for the dying;

Men of Lexington, Yorktown, Lake Erie, and the Alamo,

Sheridan's riders and Roosevelt's, statesmen and presidents;

Souls of the opening West, of deeds and visions,

Of ships and spars, cities and turbulent markets,

Of hot desires—dreamers—creators of the future—

Lovers of American sunshine, American shadow.

All of them—all—are forever enwrapped in our will,

Deathless voters, unburied voices of freedom,

Invisible leaders, teachers of new generations,

The living saviors within us—the American dead.

Here in ourselves they exist, here they are carried

Downward into the darkness of lost horizons—

Or onward into the infinite vision of man.

Let us live, therefore, in the name of those who have fallen,

That in our lives they may be resurrected:

Let us search for the light by which to find them

Within ourselves and in one another . . .
Let us uncover the graves . . . Let us pray . . .

Bright, but secret, Brother of mankind,
Whom we imagined in the reckless void:
Here in the broken bodies of our sons
We see at last what was invisible—
The remaining hope that animates the world,
The brotherhood of all men, everywhere.
This is Your Being, Your eternal Self,
Your Presence in our hearts—a meeting ground,
Wherefore so dimly lit we cannot know,
But absolute when we discover it—
The place of brotherhood, where we must walk
Fearlessly, in the darkness of the mind.
Here freedom had its origin, and here,
If anywhere, freedom will be preserved
Upon the earth, for us or other men.
It is the test of freedom in our time
To know this place and keep it for the world.

Spirit of Man: Founder of Liberty:
Great light for which democracy exists!

America is the land that You have loved:

On us the burden falls to lead the nations

Out of this frightful wilderness of steel;

On us depends the course of that which is

To come hereafter—whether freedom was

A stolen dream from Heaven, or is the truth

On which to found the future of mankind.

Brother of all races and all creeds!

If there is anything that we can do,

Now let us do it! If there is any price

That will repurchase from the hungry past

The honor of our dead, let us pay it now!

If, by resolution, we who live

Can reinspire the faint and mangled truths

Of human liberty, let us henceforth

Be as resolved and desperate in our course

As the immense and undeflected stars

That travel down the channels of Your Will!

And if, within the ancient universe,

There yet remains one spark of charity,

Brother, give us that spark, that by its light

We may reread the chapter of our time,

And from this flickering chronicle relearn

The truths that might have been self-evident.

·IV·

THE Spirit moves us onward. None may rest.
Thought presses thought: we were not born to wait.
The future crowds the ever-opening gate
Of time, and is possessed
And written in the histories of men.
The rising generations are impressed
For service in the hidden and untried;
And each, by deed or word, by gun or pen,
Must venture, must decide,
For good or evil, what is destiny.
We cannot wait—in this we are not free.
The Spirit flows within us like a tide
Upon a nameless sea,
Pulled onward by some moon we cannot know
To inundate some shore that cannot be;
Some country out of mind, beyond surmise,
Beyond the reach of sine or ratio,
Or touch or taste or smell, or ears or eyes;
Some truth we cannot dream or analyze,
Forever hidden from intelligence,

Of which our will is yet the embryo.
We cannot hold this tide. It drives us on.
It drives us ever hence,
To war and devastation more intense
Where man will fight his own automaton;
Or else, to that which waits within the heart,
Still uncomposed in time, still unordained—
The brotherhood of man—the Oregon
Of freedom won by industry and art,
By science brought to life, by law maintained.

My country will be generous to the bold:
To those who do not fear the dangerous thrust
Of progress toward the far and unforetold,
But know that like a promise freedom must
Lie forward of the darkness, not behind,
And know the Brother in their hearts, and trust
This Light at last to liberate mankind.
If they who search the void with telescopes
Can see this Light, whatever else they find;
If in the mazes of the isotopes
Where life itself lies just beyond the view,
Or in the magic genes, where science gropes

For the control of eye and hair and hue—
If everywhere we search immensity
We know that God is in us, and is true,
However dimly: then we shall be free.

Then will the myth of Nothing abdicate,
So that our works and sciences may be
The servants, not the masters, of our fate—
The lenses, not the shutters, of our light.

Then will our instruments illuminate,
And not reflect, the specters of the night,
And we shall find that which has lived unseen
In all men always—yellow, black, or white—

The shape of love, the mystic Nazarene
Who walks upon the waters of the soul.
Then will the thrust of engine and machine,
The energy of river, oil, and coal,

The clever spindles and the spiraled gears,
The switches, valves, and throttles that control
Titanic voltages and atmospheres—
All this expanse of energy and plan—

Stretch out before us, like the old frontiers,
To use and master in the name of man.
Freedom must generate in progress—this

Is what it means to be American.

The vision that the world is waiting is

The same that traced its way in wagon-tracks

Across empurpled plain and precipice,

And whispered in the starlit tamaracks

Where travelers told of freedom in the West

Around the fires of hopeful bivouacs:

The vision of a mighty purpose, pressed

By all the peoples of the earth, to make

The hidden truth within them manifest:

And as this continent was free to take,

And thus awoke the hope of all mankind,

So now, in hope, we hear the future break

On the unsovereigned beaches of the mind.

From science there is liberty to win:

The liberty of vision for the blind;

The liberty of ray and vitamin

And serum—drugs to break the peonage

To pain—and plasma and penicillin

And antitoxin and bacteriophage:

The secret properties of gland and cell,

The seeds and shadows of another age.

And liberty rings also like a bell,

Still distantly, but with familiar strain,
Where science gropes through atoms to compel
Their service as conveyers of the brain,
Or breaks the prison bars of time and space
With supersonic rocket, shell, and plane,
Or blasts electrons from their ordered place
In the interstices of destiny.
Here is a mighty continent, to face,
To open, to develop, and to free,
The virgin country of the intellect,
The far and many-tongued fraternity:
Which men of other times could not expect
This side of myth, or Milton's shadowy eyes,
But now is ours to open and project
In mountainous shapes that men can recognize
Along the shorelines of the possible.
This is the land of those who utilize
The love that acts within them like the pull
Of star to star, planet to satellite;
The love of man to man, the powerful,
The mystic source of freedom's every right,
Which signals across bloody battlefields
For us the weary peoples to unite.

It is no easy shore. Adventure yields
To mockery, which arms the prejudiced;
To wealth and all the power that it wields;
To cynic, misanthrope, and atheist:
They will not know the truth who cannot bear
The pain of love, nor will their deeds persist,
Nor will their standard, lifted anywhere,
Protect the earth from bloody dreams of hate:
But only those with courage to prepare
The chamber of the heart will celebrate
The wedding-day of truth and liberty.
This is the needle's eye, the narrow gate,
That leads beyond the horizons that we see,
To what has never been, but yet will be.

My country loves the lovers of her flag:
The strong, oracular emblem of her will—
The spangled cloth of peace—the bloody rag
Above embattled gulch and smoking hill,
Like freedom nailed in pain against the sky.
O flag, most beautiful, most versatile
Of all the banners men have lifted high,
Bright promise which the winds articulate,

Great seal of freedom, raised to certify
That man is fit to love and liberate!
Spread over us the shadow of your bars,
Projected from the authors of our state,
The red for courage like the heart of Mars,
The white between the red for liberty;
And shed the light of multiplying stars
Out of the blue, majestic mystery
Of union under God, across the earth—
The blue of Heaven, which is loyalty.
Whatever we are worth, this flag is worth.
Whatever we may dare to dream, or do,
We live in it, as it in us, from birth:
Our will is cast in red and white and blue.
Let us not make of it, for bargainers,
A rich and unregenerate parvenu
Among the empires and their connoisseurs;
But as a universal sign to man,
Raise it above the states and ministers
To show that freedom, called American,
Is carried for all peoples in our trust.
My flag is bound by no meridian:
Its realm is transcendental and august;

It represents the hand of God within
All creatures of the water and the dust.
All nations made my flag—the Pole, the Finn,
The English and the Irish and the Swede;
The Czech, who found in it his origin,
The glowing French, who helped to build its creed:
All nations, north and south, the light, the dark,
Are in this flag and cannot now secede;
Nor yet can we, the guardians of the spark,
Betray their freedom in our own behalf.
Unless we free those lands this flag will mark
America as freedom's cenotaph,
Where faith for all the world was lost, and hope
Was hauled at dusk forlornly down the staff.
It is not ours: we cannot bound its scope!
What we have borrowed we must now return
To live in earth's revolving envelope
Which wings surmount and slow propellers churn:
We must pass back the fire they passed to us,
That it may freshen and forever burn:
To those who live among the hideous
Ruins of fear, revenge, and phobia,

Haunting their fallen hopes—cadaverous,
Bereft, and lonely for America—
Along the northern sea, or on the Rhone,
Or down the sad, majestic Vltava.
O priceless flag! Immense and sacred loan
From Heaven, which the earth cannot confine!
Raised first upon the Ranger's staff, and flown
Above the muskets of the Brandywine:
Bright shred of Gettysburg and Belleau Wood,
Spirit of Tárawa and Kwajalein:
Symbol of struggle pitched in brotherhood,
And many sovereigns held in unity:
Old Glory! Guard the hopeful and the good,
And lead us onward, unconfusedly,
That in our freedom others may be free!

America is not a land of ease.
We cannot live upon this soil enwrapped
In the sweet safety of cerulean seas:
Our multi-tongued, Hesperian shores are lapped
By war and discord, breaking in from time—
The mounting swells of human struggle, capped

With envy, hate, rapacity, and crime.

But ever outward, over all the earth,

Where deserts wait the skulls, or eagles climb,

We must put forth the products of our birth;

Our faith, our laws, the meaning of our will;

Our aeroplanes to weave a magic girth

Across the continents, to trade or kill;

Our bright machines, our medicines, our bread,

Our tireless vessels, armed or mercantile;

Our boys, our lovers and our loved; our dead,

Who mark the beaches of democracy:

Put forth, not as in conquest, but to spread

Assurance of a world community,

From lone Ascension Island's foaming shore,

Across Uganda, to the ancient sea,

And on, from Basra, through the eastern door

With life and labor from the Chesapeake;

To Prestwick, where the Hornet engines roar

Like freedom, in from icy Reykjavik;

To coral isles and Polynesian joy;

Or through the fog to touch the future's cheek,

The cold and desolate slopes of Stanovoi.

Freedom is not an empty word: it springs

From hands in Arkansas and Illinois.

Its being is in men and thoughts and things
Forever borne on keels and silver wings.

America lives in her simple homes:
The weathered door, the old wisteria vine,
The dusty barnyard where the rooster roams,
The common trees like elm and oak and pine:
In furniture for comfort, not for looks,
In names like Jack and Pete and Caroline,
In neighbors you can trust, and honest books,
And peace, and hope, and opportunity.
She lives like destiny in Mom, who cooks
On gleaming stoves her special fricassee,
And jams and cakes and endless apple pies.
She lives in Pop, the family referee,
Absorbing Sunday news with heavy eyes;
And in the dog, and in the shouting kids
Returning home from school, to memorize
The history of the ancient pyramids.
And still she lives in them when darkness wakes
The distant smells and infinite katydids,
And valleys seem like black and fearsome lakes
Guarded by windows of American light,

While in the wind the family maple rakes

The lucent stars westward across the night.

And still, however far her sons may go,

To venture or to die beyond her sight,

These little windows shine incognito

Across incredulous humanity;

That all the peoples of the earth may know

The embattled destination of the free—

Not peace, not rest, not pleasure—but to dare

To face the axiom of democracy:

Freedom is not to limit, but to share;

And freedom here is freedom everywhere.

My Country was designed by Margaret Evans and Helen Gentry, set in type by Westcott & Thomson, Inc., printed by the Commanday-Roth Company, Inc., and bound by the H. Wolff Book Manufacturing Co., Inc.

DATE DUE